THE 3-MINUTE GRATITUDE JOURNAL FOR KIDS

Teaching Children Gratitude & Mindfulness

Kelly Grace

Copyright © 2020 Grace Love Publishing, LLC

All rights reserved.

No part of this book may be reproduced or used in any manner without written permission from the copyright owner except for the use of quotations in a book review.

For more information contact: **kelly@kellygracebooks.com**

ISBN: 978-1-952394-05-8 (Paperback)

www.kellygracebooks.com

THIS 3-MINUTE GRATITUDE JOURNAL BELONGS TO:

_____

Introduction:

I'm so excited that you have picked up this gratitude journal for kids! If you have never kept a gratitude journal before, it is a place where you can keep track of things about yourself and what you experienced throughout your day. Whenever you use this journal, you will get a chance to express yourself and make your thoughts and feelings known.

It is encouraged that parents help their children complete their journal entries daily.

Use the definitions below as a guide for completing the journal entries and activities.

Confidence: Feeling sure of yourself and your abilities. *(For example- Continue shooting the basketball until you make the shot.)*

Courage: Being brave and having the strength to do something. *(For example- Taking a chance and ride your bicycle for the first time without training wheels.)*

Gratitude: Focusing on what is good and being thankful for the things we have, such as having a place to live, food, friends, and family. *(For example- Thanking your mom for baking your favorite cake.)*

Kindness: Showing concern about the well-being and feelings of others. *(For example- Helping a friend up after your friend tripped and fell on the playground.)*

Overcome: To win a victory over through great effort. *(For example- Overcoming your fear of heights by going across the monkey bars.)*

Let me show you an example of how to complete the journal. (SEE NEXT PAGE)

Date: S M T (W) TH F S   01/01/20

TODAY, I FEEL:

TODAY, I AM GRATEFUL FOR:

1. My Mom
2. My Health
3. My Friends

DESCRIBE YOUR DAY USING ONE WORD.

Great

WHAT WAS THE BEST PART OF YOUR DAY?

Write or draw about it!

I made a new friend.

YOU ARE SMART!
YOU ARE IMPORTANT!
YOU ARE BRAVE!
YOU ARE POWERFUL!
YOU ARE KIND!
YOU ARE SPECIAL!
YOU ARE GENEROUS!
YOU ARE AMAZING!

Date: S M T W TH F S   ___/___/___

TODAY, I FEEL:

TODAY, I AM GRATEFUL FOR:

1. _____
2. _____
3. _____

DESCRIBE YOUR DAY USING ONE WORD.
_____

WHAT WAS THE BEST PART OF YOUR DAY?
Write or draw about it!

Date: S M T W TH F S ___/___/___

TODAY, I FEEL: 😀 🙂 😐 😟 😠

3 POSITIVE WORDS TO DESCRIBE MYSELF:

1. I AM _____
2. I AM _____
3. I AM _____

DESCRIBE THE WEATHER TODAY IN ONE WORD.

_____

WHAT WAS THE BEST PART OF YOUR DAY?
Write or draw about it!

Date: S M T W TH F S   __/__/__

TODAY, I FEEL: 😃 🙂 😐 😟 😠

TODAY, I LEARNED:

_____
_____
_____

THIS PERSON MADE MY DAY:
_____

WHAT WAS THE BEST PART OF YOUR DAY?
Write or draw about it!

Acts of Gratitude

Draw a picture in the frame below of the people for whom you are most thankful for.

Date: S M T W TH F S   __/__/__

TODAY, I FEEL:

3 POSITIVE WORDS TO DESCRIBE MYSELF:

1. I AM _____
2. I AM _____
3. I AM _____

DESCRIBE YOUR DAY USING ONE WORD.
_____

WHAT WAS THE BEST PART OF YOUR DAY?
Write or draw about it!

Date: S M T W TH F S   ___/___/___

TODAY, I FEEL:

TODAY, I LEARNED:

_____
_____
_____

DESCRIBE THE WEATHER TODAY IN ONE WORD.
_____

WHAT WAS THE BEST PART OF YOUR DAY?
Write or draw about it!

Date: S M T W TH F S   ___/___/___

TODAY, I FEEL:

TODAY, I AM GRATEFUL FOR:

1. _____
2. _____
3. _____

THIS PERSON BROUGHT ME JOY TODAY:
_____

WHAT WAS THE BEST PART OF YOUR DAY?
Write or draw about it!

What Is Gratitude?

What does gratitude mean to you? Write your definition below.

Gratitude means...

_____

_____

_____

_____

Date: S M T W TH F S   __/__/__

TODAY, I FEEL: 😃 🙂 😐 😟 😠

SOMETHING AWESOME THAT HAPPENED TODAY WAS:

_____

_____

_____

DESCRIBE YOUR DAY USING ONE WORD.

_____

WHAT WAS THE BEST PART OF YOUR DAY?
Write or draw about it!

Date: S M T W TH F S   ___/___/___

TODAY, I FEEL: 😃 🙂 😐 😟 😠

I AM THANKFUL I LEARNED HOW TO DO THIS TODAY.

_____

_____

_____

THIS PERSON BROUGHT ME JOY TODAY:

_____

WHAT WAS THE BEST PART OF YOUR DAY?
Write or draw about it!

Date: S M T W TH F S   ___/___/___

TODAY, I FEEL: 😃 🙂 😐 😟 😠

TODAY, I AM GRATEFUL FOR:

1. _____
2. _____
3. _____

DESCRIBE THE WEATHER TODAY IN ONE WORD.
_____

WHAT WAS THE BEST PART OF YOUR DAY?
Write or draw about it!

What Is Kindness?

What does kindness mean to you? Write your definition below.

Kindness means...

Date: S M T W TH F S   __ /__ /__

TODAY, I FEEL:

TODAY, I AM GRATEFUL FOR:

1. _____
2. _____
3. _____

THIS PERSON MADE MY DAY:
_____

WHAT WAS THE BEST PART OF YOUR DAY?
Write or draw about it!

Date: S M T W TH F S   ___/___/___

TODAY, I FEEL: 😀 🙂 😐 😟 😠

SOMETHING AWESOME THAT HAPPENED TODAY WAS:

_____

_____

_____

DESCRIBE THE WEATHER TODAY IN ONE WORD.

_____

WHAT WAS THE BEST PART OF YOUR DAY?
Write or draw about it!

Date: S M T W TH F S   ___/___/___

TODAY, I FEEL:

THIS IS HOW I SHOWED KINDNESS TODAY:

_____
_____
_____

DESCRIBE YOUR DAY USING ONE WORD.
_____

WHAT WAS THE BEST PART OF YOUR DAY?
Write or draw about it!

What Is Confidence?

What does confidence mean to you? Write your definition below.

Confidence means...

_____

_____

_____

_____

Date: S M T W TH F S   ___/___/___

TODAY, I FEEL:

TODAY, I AM GRATEFUL FOR:

1. _____
2. _____
3. _____

DESCRIBE THE WEATHER TODAY IN ONE WORD.

_____

WHAT WAS THE BEST PART OF YOUR DAY?
Write or draw about it!

Date: S M T W TH F S   ___/___/___

TODAY, I FEEL:

3 FRIENDS WHO ADD POSITIVITY TO MY LIFE ARE:

1. _____
2. _____
3. _____

THIS PERSON BROUGHT ME JOY TODAY:

_____

WHAT WAS THE BEST PART OF YOUR DAY?
Write or draw about it!

Date: S   M   T   W   TH   F   S   ___/___/___

TODAY, I FEEL: 😃 🙂 😐 😟 😠

SOMETHING AWESOME THAT HAPPENED TODAY WAS:

_____

_____

_____

DESCRIBE YOUR DAY USING ONE WORD.
_____

WHAT WAS THE BEST PART OF YOUR DAY?
Write or draw about it!

If I could do anything in the world right now, it would be...

(Write and draw about it!)

Date: S M T W TH F S ___/___/___

TODAY, I FEEL:

THIS IS HOW I SHOWED KINDNESS TODAY:

_____

_____

_____

DESCRIBE THE WEATHER TODAY IN ONE WORD.

_____

WHAT WAS THE BEST PART OF YOUR DAY?
Write or draw about it!

Date: S M T W TH F S   __/__/__

TODAY, I FEEL: 😃 🙂 😐 😟 😠

THIS IS HOW I SHOWED PATIENCE TODAY:

_____
_____
_____

THIS PERSON MADE MY DAY:
_____

WHAT WAS THE BEST PART OF YOUR DAY?
Write or draw about it!

Date: S M T W TH F S   ___/___/___

TODAY, I FEEL:

TODAY, I AM GRATEFUL FOR:

1. _____
2. _____
3. _____

DESCRIBE YOUR DAY USING ONE WORD.
_____

WHAT WAS THE BEST PART OF YOUR DAY?
Write or draw about it!

Acts of Gratitude

Write a thank you note to someone and give it to them.

Date: S M T W TH F S   ___/___/___

TODAY, I FEEL: 😀 🙂 😐 😟 😠

3 THINGS THAT MADE ME HAPPY TODAY ARE:

1. _____
2. _____
3. _____

I BROUGHT THIS PERSON JOY TODAY:
_____

WHAT WAS THE BEST PART OF YOUR DAY?
Write or draw about it!

Date: S M T W TH F S   __ / __ / __

TODAY, I FEEL:

TODAY, I LEARNED:

_____
_____
_____

DESCRIBE YOUR DAY USING ONE WORD.
_____

WHAT WAS THE BEST PART OF YOUR DAY?
Write or draw about it!

Date: S M T W TH F S ___/___/___

TODAY, I FEEL:

THIS IS HOW I GAINED CONFIDENCE TODAY:

_____

_____

_____

DESCRIBE THE WEATHER TODAY IN ONE WORD.

_____

WHAT WAS THE BEST PART OF YOUR DAY?
Write or draw about it!

Grateful Behavior

Some of these activities are examples of gratitude, while others are not. If the activity demonstrates gratitude, write "Y" for yes. If it does not, write "N" for no.

_____ 1. Giving food to those in need

_____ 2. Acting greedily

_____ 3. Yelling to get your way

_____ 4. Drawing a picture for your parents

_____ 5. Giving a gift to a friend

_____ 6. Not sharing your toys

_____ 7. Telling your parents, you appreciate them

_____ 8. Giving flowers to your grandparents

_____ 9. Stealing something

_____ 10. Telling someone how much they mean to you

_____ 11. Writing a "thank you" note for your teacher

_____ 12. Donating toys to kids in need

Date: S M T W TH F S   __ /__ /__

TODAY, I FEEL:

TODAY, I AM GRATEFUL FOR:

1. _____
2. _____
3. _____

THIS PERSON MADE MY DAY:

_____

WHAT WAS THE BEST PART OF YOUR DAY?
Write or draw about it!

Date: S M T W TH F S   __ / __ / __

TODAY, I FEEL:

TODAY, I LEARNED:

_____
_____
_____

I BROUGHT THIS PERSON JOY TODAY:
_____

WHAT WAS THE BEST PART OF YOUR DAY?
Write or draw about it!

Date: S M T W TH F S   __/__/__

TODAY, I FEEL: 😃 🙂 😐 😟 😠

THIS IS HOW I SHOWED KINDNESS TODAY:

_____

_____

_____

DESCRIBE YOUR DAY USING ONE WORD.

_____

WHAT WAS THE BEST PART OF YOUR DAY?
Write or draw about it!

DREAM BIG

Date: S M T W TH F S   __ /__ /__

TODAY, I FEEL: 😃 🙂 😐 😟 😠

SOMETHING I LIKE ABOUT MYSELF IS:

_____

_____

_____

THIS PERSON BROUGHT ME JOY TODAY:

_____

WHAT WAS THE BEST PART OF YOUR DAY?
Write or draw about it!

Date: S M T W TH F S   __/__/__

TODAY, I FEEL: 😃 🙂 😐 😟 😠

SOMETHING NEW I TRIED TODAY WAS:

_____

_____

_____

DESCRIBE YOUR DAY USING ONE WORD.

_____

WHAT WAS THE BEST PART OF YOUR DAY?
Write or draw about it!

Date: S M T W TH F S   ___/___/___

TODAY, I FEEL: 😃 🙂 😐 😟 😠

THIS IS HOW I SHOWED CONFIDENCE TODAY:

_____
_____
_____

THIS PERSON MADE MY DAY:
_____

WHAT WAS THE BEST PART OF YOUR DAY?
Write or draw about it!

Why are you grateful for your parents?
List or draw pictures of your answer in the cloud below.

Date: S M T W TH F S   __/__/__

TODAY, I FEEL:

3 POSITIVE WORDS TO DESCRIBE MYSELF:

1. I AM _____
2. I AM _____
3. I AM _____

DESCRIBE YOUR DAY USING ONE WORD.
_____

WHAT WAS THE BEST PART OF YOUR DAY?
Write or draw about it!

Date: S M T W TH F S   __/__/__

TODAY, I FEEL: 😃 🙂 😐 😟 😠

THIS IS HOW I SHOWED CONFIDENCE TODAY:

_____
_____
_____

DESCRIBE THE WEATHER TODAY IN ONE WORD.
_____

WHAT WAS THE BEST PART OF YOUR DAY?
Write or draw about it!

Date: S M T W TH F S ___/___/___

TODAY, I FEEL: 😃 🙂 😐 😟 😠

TODAY, I LEARNED:

_____
_____
_____

THIS PERSON BROUGHT ME JOY TODAY:
_____

WHAT WAS THE BEST PART OF YOUR DAY?
Write or draw about it!

WHAT IS YOUR FAVORITE ACTIVITY TO DO?
(Draw a picture below.)

Date: S M T W TH F S   __/__/__

TODAY, I FEEL:

TODAY, I AM GRATEFUL FOR:

1. _____
2. _____
3. _____

THIS PERSON BROUGHT ME JOY TODAY:
_____

WHAT WAS THE BEST PART OF YOUR DAY?
Write or draw about it!

Date: S M T W TH F S   __/__/__

TODAY, I FEEL: 😀 🙂 😐 😟 😠

THIS IS HOW I SHOWED KINDNESS TODAY:

_____

_____

_____

DESCRIBE YOUR DAY USING ONE WORD.

_____

WHAT WAS THE BEST PART OF YOUR DAY?
Write or draw about it!

Date: S M T W TH F S ___/___/___

TODAY, I FEEL: 😀 🙂 😐 😟 😠

SOMETHING I LIKE ABOUT MYSELF IS:

_____
_____
_____

I BROUGHT THIS PERSON JOY TODAY:
_____

WHAT WAS THE BEST PART OF YOUR DAY?
Write or draw about it!

Acts of Gratitude

Do something kind for someone else today.
Draw a picture of what you did.

Date: S M T W TH F S   __ / __ / __

TODAY, I FEEL: 😀 🙂 😐 😟 😠

TODAY, I LEARNED:

_____
_____
_____

DESCRIBE THE WEATHER TODAY IN ONE WORD.
_____

WHAT WAS THE BEST PART OF YOUR DAY?
Write or draw about it!

Date: S M T W TH F S   __/__/__

TODAY, I FEEL: 😃 🙂 😐 😟 😠

I LOVE MYSELF BECAUSE:

_____
_____
_____

I BROUGHT THIS PERSON JOY TODAY:

_____

WHAT WAS THE BEST PART OF YOUR DAY?
Write or draw about it!

Date: S M T W TH F S   ___/___/___

TODAY, I FEEL: 😃 🙂 😐 😟 😠

THIS IS HOW I SHOWED CONFIDENCE TODAY:

_____
_____
_____

THIS PERSON MADE MY DAY:
_____

WHAT WAS THE BEST PART OF YOUR DAY?
Write or draw about it!

Draw something that makes you happy.

Date: S M T W TH F S   __/__/__

TODAY, I FEEL: 😀 🙂 😐 😟 😠

THIS IS HOW I SHOWED KINDNESS TODAY:
_____
_____
_____

DESCRIBE YOUR DAY USING ONE WORD.
_____

WHAT WAS THE BEST PART OF YOUR DAY?
Write or draw about it!

Date: S M T W TH F S   __/__/__

TODAY, I FEEL:

TODAY, I AM GRATEFUL FOR:

1. _____
2. _____
3. _____

THIS PERSON BROUGHT ME JOY TODAY:
_____

WHAT WAS THE BEST PART OF YOUR DAY?
Write or draw about it!

Date: S M T W TH F S ___/___/___

TODAY, I FEEL: 😃 🙂 😐 😟 😠

SOMETHING AWESOME THAT HAPPENED TODAY WAS:

_____

_____

_____

I BROUGHT THIS PERSON JOY TODAY:

_____

WHAT WAS THE BEST PART OF YOUR DAY?
Write or draw about it!

Draw a picture of yourself showing off a special talent!

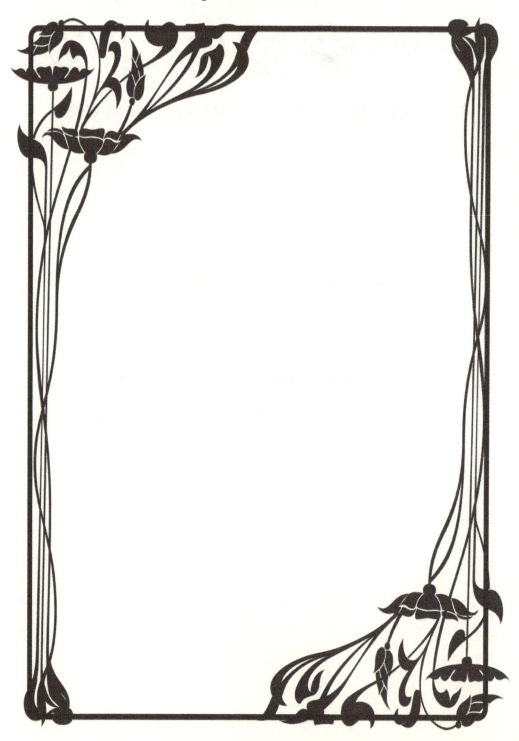

Date: S M T W TH F S   __ /__ /__

TODAY, I FEEL: 😃 🙂 😐 😟 😠

THIS IS HOW I SHOWED KINDNESS TODAY:

_____

_____

_____

DESCRIBE YOUR DAY USING ONE WORD.

_____

WHAT WAS THE BEST PART OF YOUR DAY?
Write or draw about it!

Date: S M T W TH F S   __/__/__

TODAY, I FEEL: 😃 🙂 😐 😟 😠

THIS IS HOW I SHOWED CONFIDENCE TODAY:

_____
_____
_____

THIS PERSON MADE MY DAY:
_____

WHAT WAS THE BEST PART OF YOUR DAY?
Write or draw about it!

Date: S M T W TH F S ___/___/___

TODAY, I FEEL:

TODAY, I AM GRATEFUL FOR:

1. _____
2. _____
3. _____

THIS PERSON BROUGHT ME JOY TODAY:
_____

WHAT WAS THE BEST PART OF YOUR DAY?
Write or draw about it!

Describe a time when you helped someone else.

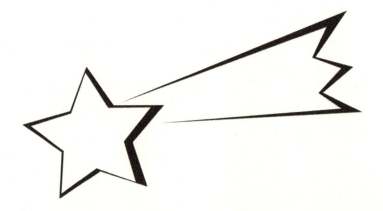

Date: S M T W TH F S   __ / __ / __

TODAY, I FEEL: 😀 🙂 😐 😟 😠

TODAY, I OVERCAME:

_____
_____
_____

DESCRIBE YOUR DAY USING ONE WORD.
_____

WHAT WAS THE BEST PART OF YOUR DAY?
Write or draw about it!

Date: S M T W TH F S   __/__/__

TODAY, I FEEL:

3 POSITIVE WORDS TO DESCRIBE MYSELF:

1. *I AM* _____
2. *I AM* _____
3. *I AM* _____

THIS PERSON BROUGHT ME JOY TODAY:
_____

WHAT WAS THE BEST PART OF YOUR DAY?
Write or draw about it!

Date: S M T W TH F S   __/__/__

TODAY, I FEEL: 😃 😊 😐 😟 😠

THIS IS HOW I SHOWED KINDNESS TODAY:

_____

_____

_____

DESCRIBE YOUR DAY USING ONE WORD.

_____

WHAT WAS THE BEST PART OF YOUR DAY?
Write or draw about it!

Draw a picture of one of your toys that you love the most.

Date: S M T W TH F S ___/___/___

TODAY, I FEEL: 😃 🙂 😐 😟 😠

THIS IS HOW I SHOWED KINDNESS TODAY:

_____

_____

_____

DESCRIBE YOUR DAY USING ONE WORD.

_____

WHAT WAS THE BEST PART OF YOUR DAY?
Write or draw about it!

Date: S M T W TH F S   ___ / ___ / ___

TODAY, I FEEL: 😀 🙂 😐 😟 😠

THIS IS HOW I SHOWED CONFIDENCE TODAY:

_____

_____

_____

THIS PERSON MADE MY DAY:

_____

WHAT WAS THE BEST PART OF YOUR DAY?

Write or draw about it!

Date: S M T W TH F S ___/___/___

TODAY, I FEEL:

TODAY, I AM GRATEFUL FOR:

1. _____
2. _____
3. _____

THIS PERSON BROUGHT ME JOY TODAY:
_____

WHAT WAS THE BEST PART OF YOUR DAY?
Write or draw about it!

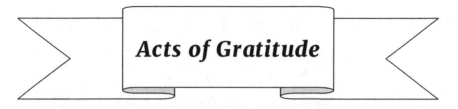

Write things in the bubbles that always make you smile!

Date: S M T W TH F S   ___/___/___

TODAY, I FEEL: 😀 🙂 😐 😟 😠

SOMETHING AWESOME THAT HAPPENED TODAY WAS:

_____

_____

_____

DESCRIBE YOUR DAY USING ONE WORD.

_____

WHAT WAS THE BEST PART OF YOUR DAY?
Write or draw about it!

Date: S M T W TH F S   ___ /___ /___

TODAY, I FEEL:

3 THINGS THAT MAKE ME HAPPY ARE:

1. _____
2. _____
3. _____

THIS PERSON MADE MY DAY:
_____

WHAT WAS THE BEST PART OF YOUR DAY?
Write or draw about it!

Date: S M T W TH F S ___/___/___

TODAY, I FEEL:

TODAY, I AM GRATEFUL FOR:

1. _____
2. _____
3. _____

DESCRIBE YOUR DAY USING ONE WORD.

_____

WHAT WAS THE BEST PART OF YOUR DAY?
Write or draw about it!

Kind Behavior

Some of these activities are examples of kindness, while others are not. If the activity demonstrates kindness, write "Y" for yes. If it does not, write "N" for no.

_____ 1. Donating toys to kids in need

_____ 2. Cheering a friend up

_____ 3. Stealing something

_____ 4. Taking turns

_____ 5. Calling someone a hurtful name

_____ 6. Inviting someone new to play with you

_____ 7. Throwing away trash that is not yours

_____ 8. Making fun of someone

_____ 9. Bringing cookies to your grandparents

_____ 10. Writing your teacher a thank you note

_____ 11. Cheating to win a game

_____ 12. Sharing your crayons

Date: S M T W TH F S   __/__/__

TODAY, I FEEL:

3 THINGS THAT MAKE ME HAPPY ARE:

1. _____
2. _____
3. _____

DESCRIBE YOUR DAY USING ONE WORD.
_____

WHAT WAS THE BEST PART OF YOUR DAY?
Write or draw about it!

Date: S M T W TH F S   __/__/__

TODAY, I FEEL: 😀 🙂 😐 😟 😠

TODAY, I LEARNED:

_____
_____
_____

DESCRIBE THE WEATHER TODAY IN ONE WORD.

_____

WHAT WAS THE BEST PART OF YOUR DAY?
Write or draw about it!

Date: S M T W TH F S   ___/___/___

TODAY, I FEEL:

3 POSITIVE WORDS TO DESCRIBE MYSELF:

1. *I AM* _____

2. *I AM* _____

3. *I AM* _____

THIS PERSON BROUGHT ME JOY TODAY:
_____

WHAT WAS THE BEST PART OF YOUR DAY?
Write or draw about it!

Who brings joy to your life and makes you happy?
(Draw a picture of you and that person.)

Date: S M T W TH F S   ___/___/___

TODAY, I FEEL: 😀 🙂 😐 😟 😠

THIS IS HOW I SHOWED KINDNESS TODAY:

_____

_____

_____

DESCRIBE YOUR DAY USING ONE WORD.

_____

WHAT WAS THE BEST PART OF YOUR DAY?
Write or draw about it!

Date: S M T W TH F S   __/__/__

TODAY, I FEEL: 😃 🙂 😐 😟 😠

SOMETHING AWESOME THAT HAPPENED TODAY WAS:

_____
_____
_____

DESCRIBE THE WEATHER TODAY IN ONE WORD.

_____

WHAT WAS THE BEST PART OF YOUR DAY?
Write or draw about it!

Date: S M T W TH F S   ___/___/___

TODAY, I FEEL:

3 POSITIVE FRIENDS I HAVE ARE:

1. _____
2. _____
3. _____

I BROUGHT THIS PERSON JOY TODAY:
_____

WHAT WAS THE BEST PART OF YOUR DAY?
Write or draw about it!

What are some positive things you can do to make someone's day better? Write them below.

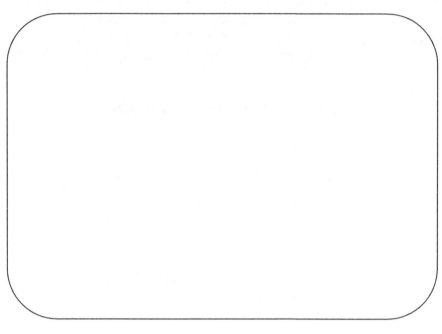

Date: S M T W TH F S   __/__/__

TODAY, I FEEL: 😃 🙂 😐 😟 😠

SOMETHING NEW I TRIED TODAY WAS:

_____

_____

_____

DESCRIBE THE WEATHER TODAY IN ONE WORD.

_____

WHAT WAS THE BEST PART OF YOUR DAY?
Write or draw about it!

Date: S M T W TH F S   ___/___/___

TODAY, I FEEL: 😃 🙂 😐 😟 😠

THIS IS HOW I SHOWED KINDNESS TODAY:

_____

_____

_____

DESCRIBE YOUR DAY USING ONE WORD.

_____

WHAT WAS THE BEST PART OF YOUR DAY?

Write or draw about it!

Date: S M T W TH F S   ___/___/___

TODAY, I FEEL:

3 PEOPLE THAT MAKE ME HAPPY ARE:

1. _____
2. _____
3. _____

THIS PERSON BROUGHT ME JOY TODAY:
_____

WHAT WAS THE BEST PART OF YOUR DAY?
Write or draw about it!

My Feelings: Pride!

I am proud of myself because _____
_____

I know I matter because _____
_____
_____

I can handle it when _____
_____
_____

Date: S M T W TH F S   __/__/__

TODAY, I FEEL: 😃 🙂 😐 😟 😠

TODAY, I LEARNED:

_____

_____

_____

I BROUGHT THIS PERSON JOY TODAY:

_____

WHAT WAS THE BEST PART OF YOUR DAY?
Write or draw about it!

Date: S M T W TH F S   __ /__ /__

TODAY, I FEEL: 😃 🙂 😐 😟 😠

THIS IS HOW I SHOWED KINDNESS TODAY:

_____

_____

_____

DESCRIBE YOUR DAY USING ONE WORD.

_____

WHAT WAS THE BEST PART OF YOUR DAY?
Write or draw about it!

Date: S M T W TH F S   __/__/__

TODAY, I FEEL:

THIS IS HOW I SHOWED CONFIDENCE TODAY:

_____

_____

_____

THIS PERSON BROUGHT ME JOY TODAY:

_____

WHAT WAS THE BEST PART OF YOUR DAY?
Write or draw about it!

If you could invent something one day, what would it be?
(Draw a picture below.)

Date: S M T W TH F S ___/___/___

TODAY, I FEEL:

3 THINGS THAT MAKE ME HAPPY ARE:

1. _____
2. _____
3. _____

DESCRIBE YOUR DAY USING ONE WORD.

_____

WHAT WAS THE BEST PART OF YOUR DAY?
Write or draw about it!

Date: S M T W TH F S   __ /__ /__

TODAY, I FEEL: 😃 🙂 😐 😟 😠

SOMETHING I LIKE ABOUT MYSELF IS:

_____

_____

_____

THIS PERSON BROUGHT ME JOY TODAY:

_____

WHAT WAS THE BEST PART OF YOUR DAY?
Write or draw about it!

Date: S M T W TH F S   __/__/__

TODAY, I FEEL:

SOMETHING NEW I TRIED TODAY WAS:

_____
_____
_____

I BROUGHT THIS PERSON JOY TODAY:

_____

WHAT WAS THE BEST PART OF YOUR DAY?
Write or draw about it!

GRATITUDE SCAVENGER HUNT

Write your answers to the things you are grateful for, for each statement listed below.

SOMETHING I'M GRATEFUL FOR

In my home is…	
In the classroom is…	
In nature is…	
That makes me laugh is…	
That makes me think is…	
That brings me joy is…	
That provides friendship is…	
That makes me feel strong is…	
That shows vibrant colors is…	
That represents my culture is…	
That is food and tastes good is…	
That I recently learned is…	

Date: S M T W TH F S   __/__/__

TODAY, I FEEL: 😀 🙂 😐 😟 😠

THIS IS HOW I SHOWED KINDNESS TODAY:

_____

_____

_____

DESCRIBE YOUR DAY USING ONE WORD.

_____

WHAT WAS THE BEST PART OF YOUR DAY?
Write or draw about it!

Date: S M T W TH F S   __/__/__

TODAY, I FEEL: 😃 🙂 😐 😟 😠

SOMETHING AWESOME THAT HAPPENED TODAY WAS:

_____

_____

_____

THIS PERSON MADE MY DAY:

_____

WHAT WAS THE BEST PART OF YOUR DAY?
Write or draw about it!

Date: S M T W TH F S   ___/___/___

TODAY, I FEEL:

TODAY, I AM GRATEFUL FOR:

1. _____
2. _____
3. _____

I BROUGHT THIS PERSON JOY TODAY:

_____

WHAT WAS THE BEST PART OF YOUR DAY?
Write or draw about it!

Gratitude Quilt

Draw and color something you are grateful for, inside the quilt square.

Date: S M T W TH F S   __/__/__

TODAY, I FEEL:

TODAY, I LEARNED:

_____
_____
_____

DESCRIBE YOUR DAY USING ONE WORD.
_____

WHAT WAS THE BEST PART OF YOUR DAY?
Write or draw about it!

Date: S M T W TH F S   __/__/__

TODAY, I FEEL: 😃 🙂 😐 😟 😠

THIS IS HOW I SHOWED KINDNESS TODAY:

_____

_____

_____

I BROUGHT THIS PERSON JOY TODAY:

_____

WHAT WAS THE BEST PART OF YOUR DAY?
Write or draw about it!

Date: S M T W TH F S   __/__/__

TODAY, I FEEL:

TODAY, I OVERCAME:

_____

_____

_____

THIS PERSON BROUGHT ME JOY TODAY:

_____

WHAT WAS THE BEST PART OF YOUR DAY?
Write or draw about it!

What Does Kindness Look Like?

Write or draw what it looks like in the space below.

At home	**At school**
With my friends	**In my community**

Date: S M T W TH F S   __/__/__

TODAY, I FEEL:

TODAY, I AM GRATEFUL FOR:

1. _____
2. _____
3. _____

THIS PERSON BROUGHT ME JOY TODAY:
_____

WHAT WAS THE BEST PART OF YOUR DAY?
Write or draw about it!

Date: S M T W TH F S ___/___/___

TODAY, I FEEL:

3 POSITIVE WORDS TO DESCRIBE MYSELF:

1. I AM _____
2. I AM _____
3. I AM _____

DESCRIBE YOUR DAY USING ONE WORD.
_____

WHAT WAS THE BEST PART OF YOUR DAY?
Write or draw about it!

Date: S M T W TH F S   __ /__ /__

TODAY, I FEEL: 😃 🙂 😐 😟 😠

TODAY, I LEARNED:

_____

_____

_____

I BROUGHT THIS PERSON JOY TODAY:
_____

WHAT WAS THE BEST PART OF YOUR DAY?
Write or draw about it!

Write down 3 of the funniest things anyone has ever said to you!

SPREAD HAPPINESS
AND SHARE LAUGHTER
WITH SOMEONE
TODAY!

Date: S M T W TH F S   __ /__ /__

TODAY, I FEEL: 😃 🙂 😐 😟 😠

THIS IS HOW I SHOWED KINDNESS TODAY:

_____

_____

_____

DESCRIBE YOUR DAY USING ONE WORD.

_____

WHAT WAS THE BEST PART OF YOUR DAY?

Write or draw about it!

Date: S M T W TH F S   __/__/__

TODAY, I FEEL:

3 POSITIVE FRIENDS I HAVE ARE:

1. _____
2. _____
3. _____

I BROUGHT THIS PERSON JOY TODAY:
_____

WHAT WAS THE BEST PART OF YOUR DAY?
Write or draw about it!

Date: S M T W TH F S   __/__/__

TODAY, I FEEL:

3 POSITIVE WORDS TO DESCRIBE MYSELF:

1. *I AM* _____
2. *I AM* _____
3. *I AM* _____

DESCRIBE YOUR DAY USING ONE WORD.

_____

WHAT WAS THE BEST PART OF YOUR DAY?
Write or draw about it!

Imagine you are writing a thank you note to yourself. What are 3 things you can thank yourself for?

Date: S M T W TH F S   __/__/__

TODAY, I FEEL: 😃 🙂 😐 😟 😠

THIS IS HOW I SHOWED CONFIDENCE TODAY:

_____

_____

_____

I BROUGHT THIS PERSON JOY TODAY:

_____

WHAT WAS THE BEST PART OF YOUR DAY?
Write or draw about it!

Date: S M T W TH F S   __/__/__

TODAY, I FEEL:

3 THINGS I'M PROUD OF TODAY ARE:

1. _____
2. _____
3. _____

DESCRIBE THE WEATHER TODAY IN ONE WORD.
_____

WHAT WAS THE BEST PART OF YOUR DAY?
Write or draw about it!

Date: S M T W TH F S   __/__/__

TODAY, I FEEL: 😃 🙂 😐 😟 😠

THIS IS HOW I SHOWED KINDNESS TODAY:

_____

_____

_____

THIS PERSON BROUGHT ME JOY TODAY:

_____

WHAT WAS THE BEST PART OF YOUR DAY?
Write or draw about it!

How Can I Show Courage?

Write or draw what it looks like in the space below.

In the community	At school
With friends	In an emergency

Date: S M T W TH F S   ___/___/___

TODAY, I FEEL: 😃 🙂 😐 😟 😠

TODAY, I LEARNED:

_____

_____

_____

DESCRIBE YOUR DAY USING ONE WORD.

_____

WHAT WAS THE BEST PART OF YOUR DAY?
Write or draw about it!

Date: S M T W TH F S   __/__/__

TODAY, I FEEL:

TODAY, I AM GRATEFUL FOR:

1. _____
2. _____
3. _____

DESCRIBE THE WEATHER TODAY IN ONE WORD.
_____

WHAT WAS THE BEST PART OF YOUR DAY?
Write or draw about it!

Date: S M T W TH F S   ___ /___ /___

TODAY, I FEEL:

3 THINGS THAT MADE ME HAPPY TODAY ARE:

1. _____
2. _____
3. _____

THIS PERSON BROUGHT ME JOY TODAY:
_____

WHAT WAS THE BEST PART OF YOUR DAY?
Write or draw about it!

Think about a family member, and write about how they make your life better.

Date: S M T W TH F S   __/__/__

TODAY, I FEEL: 😃 🙂 😐 😟 😠

TODAY, I LEARNED:

_____
_____
_____

DESCRIBE THE WEATHER TODAY IN ONE WORD.

_____

WHAT WAS THE BEST PART OF YOUR DAY?
Write or draw about it!

Date: S M T W TH F S   ___ /___ /___

TODAY, I FEEL:

TODAY, I AM GRATEFUL FOR:

1. _____
2. _____
3. _____

DESCRIBE YOUR DAY USING ONE WORD.
_____

WHAT WAS THE BEST PART OF YOUR DAY?
Write or draw about it!

Date: S M T W TH F S ___/___/___

TODAY, I FEEL: 😃 🙂 😐 😟 😠

THIS IS HOW I SHOWED KINDNESS TODAY:

_____

_____

_____

I BROUGHT THIS PERSON JOY TODAY:

_____

WHAT WAS THE BEST PART OF YOUR DAY?
Write or draw about it!

Draw a picture of your favorite thing to do.

Date: S M T W TH F S ___/___/___

TODAY, I FEEL:

3 POSITIVE WORDS TO DESCRIBE MYSELF:

1. I AM _____
2. I AM _____
3. I AM _____

DESCRIBE YOUR DAY USING ONE WORD.
_____

WHAT WAS THE BEST PART OF YOUR DAY?
Write or draw about it!

Date: S M T W TH F S ___/___/___

TODAY, I FEEL: 😃 🙂 😐 😟 😠

TODAY, I LEARNED:

_____

_____

_____

THIS PERSON BROUGHT ME JOY TODAY:

_____

WHAT WAS THE BEST PART OF YOUR DAY?
Write or draw about it!

Date: S M T W TH F S   __/__/__

TODAY, I FEEL:

3 THINGS THAT BRINGS ME JOY ARE:

1. _____
2. _____
3. _____

DESCRIBE YOUR DAY USING ONE WORD.

_____

WHAT WAS THE BEST PART OF YOUR DAY?
Write or draw about it!

**Do a chore today without being asked.
Draw a picture of the chore you did.**

Congratulations! It has been 60 days since you started writing in this Gratitude Journal.

Think about your experiences as you have learned about gratitude and mindfulness. How has learning about these concepts helped you? Write down your thoughts.

_____
_____
_____
_____
_____
_____
_____
_____
_____
_____
_____
_____
_____
_____
_____
_____
_____
_____

Dear Readers,

Thank you for your support. I hope you enjoyed this journal with your child. If you did, please consider taking a moment to leave your feedback and review. Reviews help other readers when they are searching for books they might enjoy too.

I am forever grateful for readers like you!

Thank you,

Kelly Grace

ABOUT THE AUTHOR

Kelly Grace is an entrepreneur, educator, and author. She creates children's books that are fun, engaging, inspirational and teach lessons to children of all ages and from all backgrounds.

Connect with Kelly Grace:

Facebook: @kellygracebooks

Instagram: @kellygracebooks

Visit **www.kellygracebooks.com** to get the "Mindful Matters Activity Book" for **FREE**

Made in the USA
Monee, IL
09 July 2020